RON MILLER

STARS AND GALAXIES

WORLDS BEYOND

TWENTY-FIRST CENTURY BOOKS   MINNEAPOLIS

This book is dedicated to Matilda Rae Kutschinski.

Twenty-First Century Books
A division of Lerner Publishing Group
241 First Avenue North
Minneapolis, Minnesota 55401 U.S.A.

Website address: www.lernerbooks.com

Library of Congress Cataloging-in-Publication Data

Miller, Ron, 1947-
    Stars and galaxies / by Ron Miller.
      p.   cm. — (Worlds beyond)
    Includes bibliographical references and index.
    ISBN-13: 978–0–7613–3466–8 (lib. bdg. : alk. paper)
    ISBN-10: 0–7613–3466–1 (lib. bdg. : alk. paper)
    1. Stars—Juvenile literature. 2. Galaxies—Juvenile literature. I. Title.
  QB801.7.M55 2006
  523.8—dc22   2004030813

Manufactured in the United States of America
1 2 3 4 5 6 – DP – 11 10 09 08 07 06

CONTENTS

Chapter One
The Lights in the Sky 5

Chapter Two
The Life and Death of a Star 14

Chapter Three
Red Giants and White Dwarfs 25

Chapter Four
An Infinite Variety 38

Chapter Five
Between the Stars 53

Chapter Six
The Milky Way 60

Chapter Seven
A Universe of Galaxies 76

Chapter Eight
The Birth and Death of the Universe 83

Glossary 89
For More Information 91
Index 93

The Hopi Indian sky god depicts the points of the compass, the Sun moving through the sky, and the movement of the universe.

CHAPTER ONE

THE LIGHTS IN THE SKY

On a clear night you can see thousands of **stars** dusting the sky like a scattering of diamonds on black velvet. In the country, far from bright city lights, it might be possible to see more than 2,000 stars in the sky at any one time. While this is a rare view for most people living in the modern world, it was a common one for the ancients, for whom the sight of thousands of stars above the dark streets of Babylon, the farms of Egypt, or the plains of Persia was a most familiar one. It was an important sight, too, because the movement of the stars in the sky measured the passing seasons of the year. Life in ancient Egypt, for example, revolved around the annual flooding of the Nile, which left rich deposits of silt on the farmland that bordered the river. The rising of the bright star Sirius marked the beginning of the Egyptian year because it appeared around the same time the waters of the Nile flooded. This made the appearance of Sirius an important event. The positions of stars were of paramount importance in ancient Polynesia, too, where the ability to navigate accurately between tiny islands separated by hundreds or even thousands of

An ancient Egyptian concept of the universe shows the stars arching over the prone figure of Earth, while the Sun and Moon move in the space between.

miles of trackless ocean was a matter of life or death. The Polynesian navigators guided their ships by memorizing the positions of certain stars.

Eventually, people began asking questions about the stars. What are they? What are they made of? How far away are they?

What Are the Stars?

To most ancient peoples, the stars were points of shining light on a dome that arched over the Earth—like lamps in a vaulted ceiling. They were all considered to be about the same distance from Earth, even if some were larger and brighter than others.

A medieval astronomer and his instruments, depicted by the great German artist Albrecht Dürer

The stars are not spaced evenly in the sky, but are instead scattered randomly. So it is not surprising that out of all the stars visible to the naked eye, many should seem to form patterns. This is because the human brain is especially adept at trying to find meaningful arrangements in any kind of random pattern. Splatter some ink or paint on a sheet of white paper and you will soon be able to pick out patterns of dots that remind you of specific shapes and familiar objects. Ancient people did the same thing: They found patterns in the stars and gave them names. We still recognize many of these ancient patterns—or **constellations**—such as the Big Dipper, Orion, Pisces, and others. Different societies, of course, found different sets of patterns. The Chinese and Aztec constellations are very different from the ones identified by the Greeks and Romans.

Thousands of years ago, many people thought that these patterns had some special significance and could even influence human lives directly. They thought that because a constellation reminded them of the shape of a fish, for instance, it must have something to do with water. There are still people today who think that this is true and who believe in a **pseudoscience** called "astrology." But the truth is that the stars are randomly scattered and that any patterns they seem to make were invented entirely by the human imagination.

(7)

A medieval depiction of the Milky Way as a band of stars

Although astronomers of several thousand years ago could not determine exactly what the stars were, or even how far away they were, they were very good at observing them and measuring their positions. The Greek scholar Eratosthenes (c. 276–192 B.C.) created a catalog of the positions of 675 of the brightest stars. Hipparchus (c. 146–127 B.C.), from his observatory on the island of Rhodes, produced a catalog of 850 stars. With the fall of Western science during the Middle Ages, the advance of astronomical knowledge was taken up by the Arab world (with the result that to this day many stars bear Arabic names, such as Betelgeuse, Aldebaran, Algol, Mizar, and Deneb, among many others).

When the Italian scientist Galileo Galilei (1564–1642) pointed his newly invented telescope at the Milky Way in 1609, he observed that it was nothing but "a mass of innumerable stars planted together in clusters." Later, the British astronomer Sir William Herschel (1738–1822) theorized that the Milky Way we see from Earth is in reality a broad, flat cluster of stars, shaped something like a lens—thicker in the center than at the edges. We see this cluster, he said, as a band of stars arching through the sky because we are seeing it edge-on. Still, no one knew for certain how far away the stars were.

In 1838, a German astronomer named Friedrich Wilhelm Bessel (1784–1846) made the first measurement of the distance to a star. Using a method called **parallax measurement**, he determined that a star called 61 Cygni was 10.9 **light-years** from Earth. A light-year is the distance light travels in one year. Since light moves at the incredible speed of 186,000 miles per second

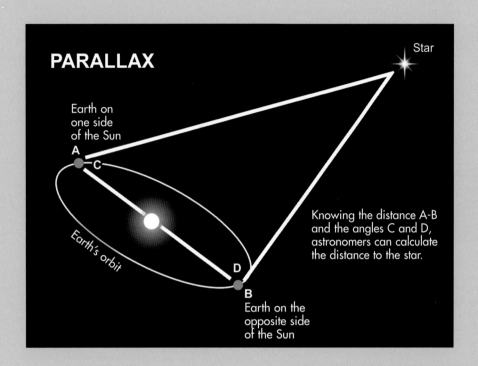

PARALLAX

Star

Earth on
one side
of the Sun

A

C

Earth's orbit

D

B

Earth on the
opposite side
of the Sun

Knowing the distance A-B
and the angles C and D,
astronomers can calculate
the distance to the star.

Hold your index finger up in front of your eyes, just in front of your nose. Now close one eye while keeping the other open. Did your finger appear to jump to one side? That is the result of parallax. This occurs when a single object is observed from two different positions—in this case, the two different positions are the result of the space that separates your eyes. Now slowly move your finger away from your nose. Every few inches stop and close an eye. You will notice that the "jump" your finger makes becomes less the farther your finger is from your eyes. You could calculate the exact distance to an object this way, by measuring the amount it jumps. (In fact, your eyes and brain do this very thing for you automatically, allowing you to judge distances quite accurately.)

If a measurement of the position of a star in the sky is made in the summer, when the Earth is on one side of the Sun, and then in the winter, when it is on the other side, astronomers have in effect seen the star with a pair of "eyes" 186 million miles apart. This tiny movement of the star is called its parallax. And just as you can judge the distance to an object by the jump it makes when seen by first one eye then the other, astronomers can calculate the exact distance to a star by measuring the jump it makes in the sky when seen from two different positions.

Sir William Herschel believed that the Milky Way was a flattened disk of stars (seen here edge-on) with the Sun (white dot in the middle) located not far from the center.

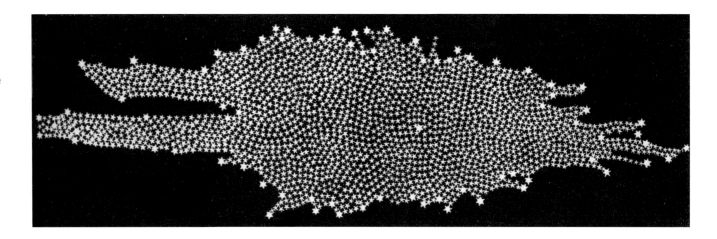

(299,330 km per second), in one year it travels some 6 trillion miles (9 trillion km)! A Scottish astronomer named Thomas Henderson (1798–1844) calculated the distance to Alpha Centauri and found that it is only 4.3 light-years away (although he made this calculation earlier than Bessel, he did not publish it until 1839). These are incredible distances. This immediately explained why the stars appear to be nothing more than points of light. Even though Alpha Centauri is the star nearest to us, it is still 277,420 times farther away than the Sun.

For millions of years human beings wondered what the stars were, never realizing that there was a star so close that it could even be seen in the daytime. This star is the Sun, of course, and any answer to the question "What is a star?" must begin with the Sun, because this was the first star to be studied closely.

The most obvious fact about the Sun is that it is very bright and very hot. For centuries, people thought that the Sun gave off heat and light because it was burning. This seemed to make sense. After all, everyone was familiar with things like fire, hot coals, and molten metal, all of which gave off heat and light just like the Sun. So it seemed reasonable to assume that the Sun, too, was burning. Eventually, however, scientists made some calculations.

Was it possible that the Sun was a vast mass of some burning material, such as coal? In 1871, the German scientist Hermann von Helmholtz (1821–1894) calculated that 1,500 pounds of coal would have to be burned on every square foot (680 kg on every 0.09 m²) of the Sun's surface every hour to produce its heat and light. He realized that no known substance—let alone coal—could burn so fast. Besides, how was enough oxygen available to support all this combustion? It was found that even if the Sun was made entirely of something as flammable as a mixture of gasoline and oxygen, it wouldn't last more than a hundred years.

In the middle of the nineteenth century, two scientists—von Helmholtz and an Englishman named William Thomson Kelvin (1824–1907)—theorized that the heat of the Sun might be caused by **gravitational collapse**. According to them, the Sun was a sphere of gas that was slowly compacting under the pressure of its own gravity. This gravitational energy was released in the form of heat. Their calculations seemed to fit all the known facts about the Sun very neatly since, according to them, such a Sun would produce light and heat for at least 30 million years.

The growth of geologic science in the nineteenth century soon showed that the Earth—and consequently the Sun—was in fact many times older than that. So there had to be a new idea about what kept the Sun hot—and this time a theory that would

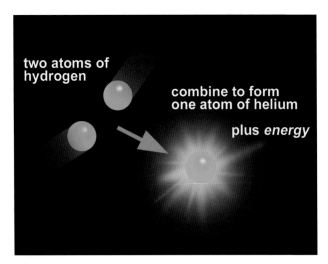

The fusion of atomic nuclei releases vast quantities of energy and is the source of the heat and light emitted by stars.

Facing Page: A cutaway view of the interior of a typical star, such as our own Sun: Radiation created deep in the core slowly makes its way to the surface, where it is finally released in the form of heat, light, and other radiation.

keep the Sun burning for billions instead of millions of years. What could possibly be the source of so much energy? This question would not be answered until the discovery of **radioactivity**.

Radioactivity was discovered at the end of the nineteenth century. Scientists realized that the **nucleus** of the **atom** stores unbelievably vast amounts of energy. They began to speculate that the source of the Sun's heat and light comes from a nuclear reaction of some sort. Temperatures and pressures at the core of the Sun would be more than sufficient to crush the nuclei of atoms together, releasing tremendous amounts of energy in the process. When energy is released by slamming two atomic nuclei together, this is called **nuclear fusion** (as opposed to **nuclear fission**, in which the nuclei of atoms are split apart).

The Sun is about three-fourths **hydrogen**, the simplest, lightest, most abundant element in the universe (about one fifth of the Sun is helium, and the remainder is heavier elements). When two hydrogen nuclei fuse together, they form the nucleus of an atom of helium. But the helium nucleus weighs a tiny fraction less than the two hydrogen nuclei separately. This tiny fraction of mass has been converted to pure energy. For every 2.2 pounds (1 kg) of hydrogen that is fused, about 0.015 pound (0.007 kg) is converted into energy—about 400 trillion trillion watts of energy. This is enough to light 10 trillion trillion 40-watt lightbulbs.

Even though the Sun converts several hundred million tons of hydrogen every second, it will still take several billion years before it is all used up. But long before that occurs, other things will happen to the Sun. . . .

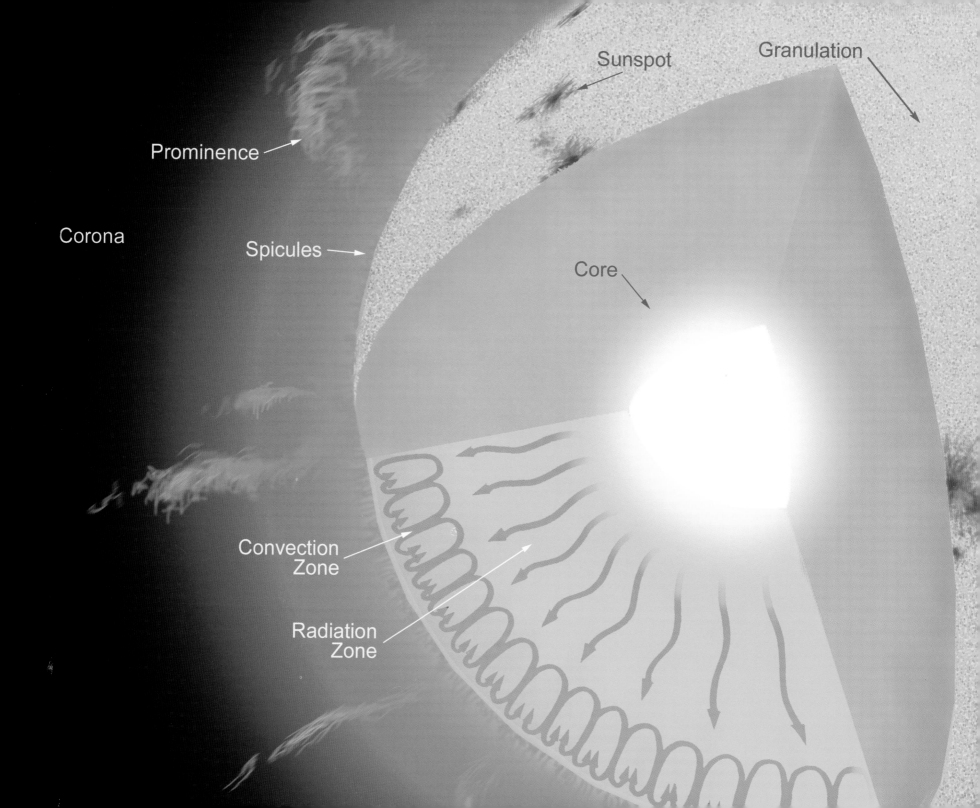

Granulation

Sunspot

Corona

Prominence

Core

Spicules

Convection
Zone

Radiation
Zone

CHAPTER TWO

THE LIFE AND DEATH OF A STAR

In the beginning was the cloud. It was a vast billow of fine dust and gas—mostly hydrogen—billions of miles wide. Our **galaxy** was filled with millions upon millions of similar clouds, some smaller and some enormously larger. A cloud like this is called a **nebula**, from the Latin word for cloud. It is cold—around −279°F (−173°C)—and very thin. Most of space is a nearly perfect **vacuum**, with only two to ten atoms, usually hydrogen, in every cubic inch (16 cm³). However, a cloud may have 10,000 atoms per cubic centimeter. While this is still nearly a vacuum—the air in the room around you contains more than 20 billion billion atoms in every 0.06 cubic inch (1 cm³)—the atoms are close enough together to collide and form **molecules**, or groups of connected atoms.

If the cloud is large enough—a few thousand times as massive as the Sun—and if it is not too hot, it slowly begins to collapse. Once the collapse starts, it cannot stop. The molecules start drifting toward the center of the cloud, where there is more material and the pull of gravity is greater. The moving molecules occasion-

(14)

ally bump against others and create a little heat. As the cloud condenses and its molecules get closer together, it grows warmer.

The knot of condensing gas in the cloud is probably just a small part of a much larger cloud. The condensation begins where the gas is a bit denser than elsewhere. It's possible that at other places in the parent cloud, other small knots of condensing gas are also forming. Any of them may eventually become stars, too.

The center of the cloud, where the gas and dust is densest, grows warm and then hot as more and more material falls into it. (If you've ever noticed a tire growing warmer as you inflate it, you've seen how a gas gets hotter as it is compressed.) As the center of the cloud becomes denser, its gravity becomes greater and it pulls even more gas and dust into it. In just one year, a cloud of gas 2,000 billion miles (3,218 billion km) wide can collapse to only 200 million miles (322 million km)—ten thousand times smaller. Soon it becomes hot enough—over 3000°F (1650°C)—to vaporize any solid grains of ice or dust. At the same time the core of the cloud grows even denser and hotter. A dim, reddish glow, like that of a hot coal, may now be visible within the densely packed cloud.

Driven by increasing heat and pressure, the atoms in the core collide with tremendous violence. After perhaps only a few thousand years, the atoms collide so violently that they knock their **electrons** out of their orbits. This process, called **ionization**, occurs at a temperature of nearly 17,000°F (9427°C). The gas, no longer composed of intact atoms, is now composed of charged particles called **ions**. These are the electrons that have been knocked free, which are negatively charged, and the nuclei, which are positively charged.

What starts the collapse of the cloud of gas in which a star is born? What gives the cloud that initial nudge? It can be almost anything—perhaps the shock wave from a nearby exploding star, called a **supernova**, occurring in much the same way that a loud noise can start an avalanche. There is some evidence for this theory. Supernova explosions create huge quantities of radioactive elements, which would not be found in the original cloud. The solar system today contains a high concentration of these rare elements. This may indicate that a supernova started the collapse of the nebula that eventually produced our solar system.

As the cloud's core continues to heat up, the nuclei begin to collide. Normally, two positively charged particles would repel each other, like the north poles of a pair of magnets. However, as the core reaches a temperature of 10–20 million°F (6–12 million°C), the nuclei are forced not only to collide but also to stick together. This is called **fusion**, a process that creates a new element—helium—one that is twice as heavy as the original hydrogen. Even more important than the creation of heavier nuclei from lighter ones is the release of energy in very large amounts.

It has taken the cloud 10 million years to contract enough for its core to reach the temperature needed for fusion to begin. The collapsing cloud of gas is only a **protostar**. But as soon as the spark of fusion is lit, it becomes a full-fledged star, running on the energy produced by fusion. This new source of energy is so much more powerful than that created by simple gravitational collapse that the process of collapse actually stops. The cloud's outward pressure now balances the inward pressure. A star has been born.

All Stars Are Not Created Equal

While all stars form in more or less the same way, the stars that result at the end of the process may be quite different from one another. The difference lies in the amount of **mass** of which the star is composed—in other words, the amount of hydrogen it contains. If we take the mass of our Sun as a standard and call it

As a cloud of dust and gas contracts under its own gravitation, it generates heat. You can see how this happens by performing a simple experiment. All that is required is a bicycle tire pump. Connect the pump to a tire (or plug the end of its hose in some way) and pump the handle a few times. Now feel the side of the pump. It will have become quite warm, perhaps even hot. The compression of the air inside the pump caused the air to become hotter. In the same way, the gases at the center of a collapsing interstellar cloud will also become hot. This same process is also the source of the internal heat of substellar objects such as brown dwarfs.

Facing page: This knot of dark gas and dust has been slowly compacting for centuries.

As the knot of dust and gas collapses, its spin will increase. The core will become hot enough to trigger a nuclear reaction, and a star will be born.

one **solar mass**, the most common mass for stars ranges from one-tenth solar mass to one solar mass. Most known stars range from one-tenth to ten solar masses. The amount of a star's mass makes a great difference in the kind of star it will be.

Stars of about the same mass as our Sun tend to resemble it in size and color. Stars with a great deal more mass are usually much larger, hotter, and brighter. A star of ten solar masses would be about five times larger than our Sun, three and a half times hotter, and 5,000 times brighter. Smaller stars tend to be cooler and dimmer. The vast majority of stars are red dwarfs, with only about one fifth the mass of the Sun. They comprise about 98 percent of the stars in our galaxy. A star only one tenth the mass of the Sun would be only 13 percent its size, about half as hot, and just one thousandth as bright. Bodies much smaller than one-tenth solar mass would not have had enough gravitational energy to light their nuclear furnaces, while stars with more than ten times the mass of the Sun would tend to explode. The upper limit to star size is 150 times the mass of the Sun.

An example of a star that is too big for its own good is one discovered by the Hubble Space Telescope. Sitting in the midst of the Pistol Nebula is the most luminous star known to astronomers. It may originally have been 200 times as massive as the Sun. As big as the orbit of Earth, it is 10 million times as powerful as the Sun, unleashing as much in six seconds as the Sun does in one year. It is consuming its fuel at such a tremendous rate that it will probably last only another 1 to 3 million years, finally disappearing in the blast of a supernova.

This little star, a **red dwarf**, has only one tenth the mass of the Sun. It is too faint and too cool to warm the frozen planets that orbit it.

β Centauri

Vega

Antares

The Sun

BIG STARS

The Sun is dwarfed by some of the largest stars.

Typical small stars in comparison to the Sun

Aldebaran

Arcturus

SMALL STARS

The Sun

Sirius B

Kruger 60 A

Proxima Centauri

Barnard's Star

(20)

Buried deep within the Pistol Nebula is the brightest star known in our galaxy. The mass that the star has ejected has formed the nebula that surrounds it.

Classifying Stars

Astronomers use a special diagram (called a **Hertzsprung-Russell diagram**, after Danish astronomer Ejnar Hertzsprung and American astronomer Henry Norris Russell, who drew the first ones in 1911 and 1913, respectively) to classify stars—in much the same way that biologists classify animals and plants. In the diagram, the vertical line is a star's brightness or luminosity, and the horizontal line is the star's temperature. The luminosity is often measured against that of the Sun, with the Sun being 1.0. When stars of many different types are plotted on the diagram, most of them fall along a line that runs roughly diagonally from the upper left corner. Astronomers call this line of stars the **main sequence**. About 90 percent of all known stars—including the Sun—lie on the main sequence.

The temperature of a star determines its **spectral class**, or color. Just as a piece of iron will go from a dull red glow to yellow heat to a dazzling white gleam as it is heated to ever-increasing temperatures, the color of stars follows the same sequence: red stars are cooler than yellow stars, and yellow stars are cooler than blue-white ones. The spectral classes are labeled O, B, and A for hot, blue stars; F and G for yellow stars; and K and M for cool, red stars. The Sun is an average G-class star.

Stars that are very cool but also very bright are **red giants**, which find a special place on the diagram. Stars that are very hot but also dim are **white dwarfs**, and they are also located in a special position.

The H-R diagram, as it is known, is a valuable tool that enables astronomers not only to compare different types of stars but to work out the evolution of a star's life. For instance, as a star evolves, its position on the diagram will change. At the end of the Sun's life, it will move into the class of red giants and then, finally, drop down to join the white dwarfs.

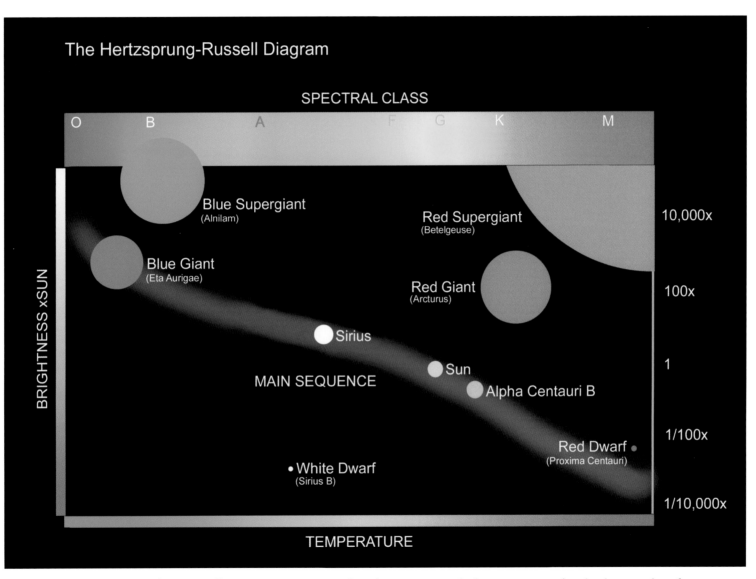

The Hertzsprung-Russell diagram allows astronomers to classify stars in much the same way that biologists classify insects and flowers.

The following table lists the fifteen stars nearest to Earth.

NAME	DISTANCE (LIGHT-YEARS)	MASS TIMES THE SUN	RADIUS TIMES THE SUN	SPECTRAL TYPE
Sun	0.0	1.0	1.0	G2
Alpha Centauri	4.3	1.1	1.2	G2
Barnard's Star	6.0	0.15	0.15	M5
Wolf 359	7.5	0.1?	0.20	M8
Lalande 21185	8.2	0.35	0.46	M2
Luyten 726-8	8.4	0.10	0.14	M6
Sirius	8.6	2.4	1.8	A1
Ross 154	9.4	0.2?	0.24	M5
Ross 248	10.2	0.2?	0.07	M6
Epsilon Eridani	10.7	0.7?	0.84	K2
Luyten 789-6	10.8	0.1?	0.11	M6
Ross 128	10.8	0.2?	0.1	M5
Epsilon Indi	11.2	0.7	0.76	K5
61 Cygni	11.4	0.6	0.72	K5
Tau Ceti	11.4	0.9	1.0	G8

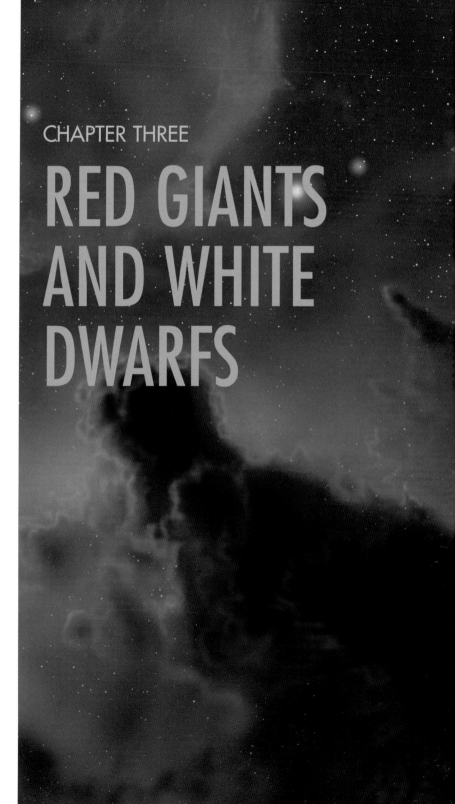

CHAPTER THREE

RED GIANTS AND WHITE DWARFS

As a star gets older, it has less fuel to convert into energy. As its hydrogen gets used up, the amount of helium in its core—the end product of hydrogen fusion—increases. As the rate at which hydrogen is being fused drops, the star is no longer able to maintain the outward pressure that counterbalances gravitational collapse. Gravity then contracts the core of the star, driving its temperature up. Eventually, the pressure and temperature become so great that the helium atoms begin to fuse into heavier elements, such as carbon. This occurs at a very high rate, so that the core begins producing energy very rapidly and becomes even hotter. This additional heat causes the outer layers of the star to expand into space. As the gases expand, they cool. The result is that the core is much hotter than it was in the original, hydrogen-burning star, while the outer atmosphere is much cooler. The new star is now not only much larger than it once was, but the part we can see from Earth—the outer atmosphere—is much cooler, and consequently redder. We call these stars red giants.

THE SUN AS A RED GIANT

Our own Sun will eventually enter a red-giant stage as it uses up the last of its hydrogen fuel. As it does, its atmosphere will expand until it engulfs the orbits of Mercury, Venus, and, finally, perhaps even that of Earth. The inner planets will be destroyed as they are overwhelmed by a flood of red-hot gas, while Earth will most likely be incinerated by a Sun hundreds of times larger than it is today. Fortunately, this event is at least 4 billion years in the future. With any luck, humankind will be living safely on the more distant worlds and moons of the solar system by then.

Billions of years from now, the Sun will expand into a red giant. As it expands past the orbit of Venus, the increased heat will boil away Earth's oceans and will eventually turn the entire surface of our planet into a sea of molten lava.

Because they are so large, red giants are very bright stars. They can shine 10,000 times more brilliantly than our own Sun. This not only makes them easy to see in the night sky, but their red color makes them very distinctive. Take Betelgeuse, for example. It is the bright star on the left shoulder of the constellation Orion. It is a huge star—800 times larger than the Sun—and even though it is 500 light-years away, it is still one of the brightest stars in the sky.

Eventually, the helium in a red giant will give out, and the star will start burning even heavier elements, such as carbon, which was the product of helium fusion. When carbon atoms are fused, they produce oxygen. When the carbon is used up, the star begins fusing the oxygen atoms, and so on, through heavier element after

The cool red giant Antares fills much of the sky as seen from this imaginary planet. Its companion, a hot blue star, can be seen high in the sky on the left.

heavier element. These last stages of a star's life occur very quickly. A star like our Sun has enough hydrogen to last about 10 billion years. But once it starts fusing heavier elements, the fuel supply may last only another thousand years.

As a red giant enters the final stages of its life, its thin, red-glowing atmosphere begins to drift off into space, blown away by its energetic core. The inner core—which still contains most of the mass of the original star—is slowly shrinking in size. As it does, it gets hotter. All the while, heavy elements are being converted into even heavier ones. Finally, most of the atomic nuclei in the core will have been converted into iron. The star can go no further than this. Iron is too stable and resists being fused into a heavier element. The star is like a chunk of coal that has burned into a cinder.

With no source of energy left to counterbalance the force of gravity, the star begins to contract rapidly. It grows smaller and denser until the **subatomic** particles that make up the core—electrons and neutrons—can be compressed no further. The star, which may have originally been the size of the Sun, is now no larger than Earth. It has become a white dwarf.

Even though the white dwarf is extremely tiny, it is still a very massive object. A single thimbleful would weigh hundreds of tons. It still retains almost all of the material contained in the original star, but this material has been compacted into a very small volume. If you have ever taken a large handful of snow and compressed it into a very small snowball, you have seen what has happened to the star. You had the same amount of snow as before, but it has now been compacted into a much smaller size.

When the star finally collapses into a white dwarf, it becomes extremely hot. The surface temperature may become greater than that of the Sun, and it will shine with an intense blue-white light. Even though this heat is produced by gravitational contraction and not nuclear processes, it will still last for a very long time . . . but, eventually, the star will cool off and become a dark, planet-sized cinder.

Other Fates

If a star is large enough, its gravity will be so great when it finally collapses that something much stranger than a white dwarf will result.

A white dwarf will be the end result of any star with a mass about 1.4 times that of the Sun or less. But if a star is more massive than that, it will collapse into a much smaller, much denser object than a white dwarf: a **neutron star**. These can be created only as the result of a supernova explosion, when almost the entire mass of the original star—a star that may already have been twice as massive as the Sun—will have been compacted into an object as small as a mile in diameter. A thimbleful of neutron star might weigh 100 million tons!

A neutron star would not look like anything normally associated with the word *star*. It would be a tiny, dimly glowing object— perhaps even cool enough for a crust of some kind to form on its surface. At first glance it might seem to resemble a small asteroid, but its true nature would be revealed by its intense gravitational field. Another clue would be the rapid rate at which it is spinning.

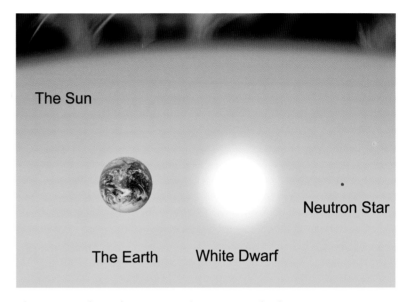

The Sun and Earth compared to a typical white dwarf and neutron star

A star spins faster and faster as it collapses and gets smaller. If you have ever seen ice skaters spinning, you have seen a similar occurrence. They start spinning with their arms held out from their body, but as they draw them in they begin to spin more quickly. If the mass of any spinning body—such as that of the spinning ice skater—is drawn toward its center, it will spin faster. The same thing happens to a neutron star. The original star may have been a slowly rotating body one million miles in diameter. But as it grows smaller, its mass moves more closely toward its middle and its spin increases. By the time it is only a few miles wide, it may be spinning several times a second. An ordinary asteroid spinning this fast would be torn apart. Only the density and intense gravitational field of the neutron star hold it together.

Beacons in Space

In 1967, Irish astronomer Jocelyn Bell Burnell was astonished to discover a flashing object in the night sky. It seemed to pulse at perfectly regular intervals, several times a second, like some sort of beacon. It was hard to imagine any natural object that could do this, and at first many scientists thought that the pulses might be signals from an extraterrestrial civilization.

It was eventually realized that what they were seeing was a very special type of neutron star that—because of its regular, metronome-like pulsing—was dubbed a **pulsar**.

Some neutron stars have very strong magnetic fields. These probably occurred when the magnetic field of the original star

Facing Page: Some neutron stars are as small as asteroids. Here is a neutron star that has wandered into a field of asteroids, some of which are being drawn into the star's powerful gravitational field and are colliding with it.

became concentrated as it shrank. In the powerful magnetic field of a neutron star, ions are accelerated to extremely high speeds. When this happens they give off **radiation**. This radiation is emitted in the form of beams that shoot in opposite directions from the spinning star. Exactly how the star forms these blazing jets is still a mystery.

As the pulsar rotates, these beams of light sweep through the sky like the beam of light from a lighthouse. And just as a lighthouse appears to blink at regular intervals, every time its beam crosses your line of vision, the rotating pulsar appears to blink in the sky.

While a pulsar's blinking is usually as regular as the ticking of a clock, there are occasional irregularities, like hiccoughs. No one knows for sure what causes these, but they may be the result of "starquakes" fracturing the solid crust, or the impact of an asteroid caught in the pulsar's tremendous gravitational field.

An Explosive Finale

While most stars will end their lives more or less as we expect the Sun to—a gradual expansion into a red giant followed by an equally, if somewhat faster, collapse into a white dwarf—other stars suffer a more violent fate. They suddenly detonate in a huge explosion that can produce as much energy in a few days as the Sun emits in 10,000 years! A star exploding this way was called a **nova**, from the Latin word for "new," by ancient astronomers, because the sudden flare-up looked as though a new star had appeared in the night sky.

A sudden outburst of energy has turned this star into a nova. It is superheating the surface of one of its planets, while radiation from the blast is creating colorful auroras in the atmosphere.

The star drawn to the left of the crescent moon in this rock painting in New Mexico may be an eyewitness record of the supernova of 1572 that created the Crab Nebula. The handprint may be the "signature" of this unknown observer.

Throughout past centuries, astronomers were puzzled by the sudden appearance of a new star in the sky. For instance, in July 1054, Chinese astronomers noted the appearance of what they called a "guest star" in the constellation Taurus. The guest star was visible in broad daylight for three weeks and could be seen at night for two years before it finally faded into invisibility. What the Chinese astronomers had witnessed was a supernova explosion.

American Indians living in Chaco Canyon, in New Mexico, may also have witnessed this impressive sight. A rock painting, or pictograph, seems to illustrate the appearance of the new star. It is shown near a crescent moon, which would have been very close to the strange new guest star at that time.

Other guest stars have been seen over the centuries. In November 1572, for instance, the Danish astronomer Tycho Brahe (1546–1601) noticed a new star in the constellation Cassiopeia. He wrote a book about what he saw called *De Nova Stella* (Latin for *About the New Star*). After that, any similar new star was called a nova. In the 1930s, astronomers discovered that there was one particular class of star that exploded with special violence. A massive explosion such as this was called a supernova.

(33)

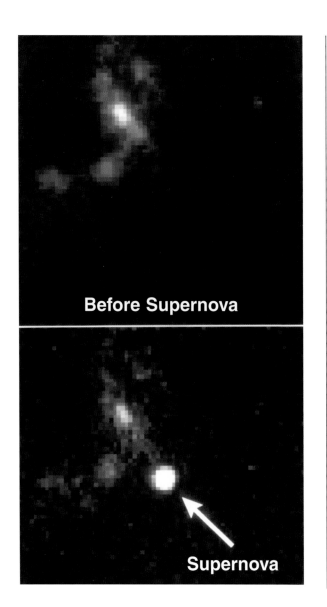

Before Supernova

Supernova

A very special set of circumstances must take place before a star can become a nova, so special that novas are very rare events indeed. Of the 100 billion stars in our galaxy, only 30 to 50 explode each year. Although there is still much to be understood about how and why novas occur, they are thought to be small, very hot stars that have binary companions. That is, they are double stars, orbiting so close to each other that even powerful telescopes cannot separate them. The more massive of the two stars grows old more quickly than the smaller companion. It enters the red giant stage, burns all of its fuel, and collapses into a white dwarf. Eventually, the smaller star also becomes a red giant. When it blows off its outer layers of gas, some of this will fall onto the older dwarf star. The expanding red giant may even totally engulf the older star. This adds fresh hydrogen fuel to it, causing huge explosions on its surface. These explosions are what we witness as novas.

For stars of about the same mass as our Sun on up to stars with six times its mass, their fate is to become white dwarfs—and the occasional nova. When a star has more than ten times the mass of the Sun, an entirely different fate awaits it. It may burst into a supernova, a titanic explosion that will cause the star to suddenly **flare** with a billion times the brightness of the Sun. For a few days, the supernova will outshine the combined stars of the entire galaxy.

What causes a star to do this is still not entirely understood. A clue may lie in the fact that there are two distinct types of super-

This distant supernova was discovered by the Hubble Space Telescope.

nova. In a Type I event, mass from one star in a binary pair is dumped onto a nearby, carbon-rich white dwarf that is near the 1.4 solar-mass limit. But instead of causing an ordinary nova burst, the entire star suddenly disappears in a single, incredible explosion. A Type II supernova may be the explosion of a star that is simply too massive to remain stable. These are stars that are more than six times as massive as the Sun. When they collapse in their old age, the tremendous pressures in their cores may trigger nuclear reactions impossible for smaller, less massive stars. These nuclear reactions may be violent enough to cause the star to explode into a supernova.

What remains after a supernova? The core of the original star, if it is more massive than 1.4 solar masses, will collapse into a neutron star. In fact, it is thought that most neutron stars are the result of supernova explosions, since only a very large, massive star would have a core as big as 1.4 solar masses, the minimum size required for creating a neutron star. Meanwhile, the atmosphere of the star is blasted out into space, often forming a beautiful shell of glowing gas.

More and More Mass

What happens to a star so large that when it explodes it leaves a core with a mass 3.5 times that of the Sun? It will collapse, of course, but it will go beyond the stage of a neutron star. It will continue to collapse, becoming smaller and smaller and ever more dense . . . until its ever-increasing gravity crushes it into that ultimate weirdness, the **black hole**.

This nebula is the still-expanding remnant of a supernova. The glowing shell of gas is all that remains of the star's outer layers.

Gravity is created by mass. Every mass in the universe, whether it be a mote of dust or a planet, attracts every other mass. The more mass, the more gravity. You and the Earth attract each other because you both possess mass, but the Earth has trillions of tons more mass than you do, so it attracts you more strongly than you attract it. The amount of gravity an object has can be described as its **escape velocity**. This is the speed at which an object would have to move to escape the body entirely. If something is launched at less than escape velocity, it will eventually fall back. The escape velocity for Earth is about 7 miles per second (11 km/sec). This is how fast a bullet would have to be fired for it never to fall back to the ground. The escape velocity for a more massive object like the Sun is about 380 miles per second (600 km/sec). To escape the surface of a black hole, an object would have to be launched at a speed of more than 186,000 miles per second (300,000 km/sec)—more than the speed of light. This means that the photons that compose a beam of light are not traveling fast enough to leave the surface of the black hole. Light may fall onto a black hole, but it can never escape.

No one has ever seen a black hole directly. It is hard to see something that can neither reflect nor emit light, but there is much evidence that it exists. There are at least two ways by which a potential black hole might be detected.

The first way is by the effect it would have on a star orbiting it. The size and velocity of a star's orbit reveal the mass of the object it is orbiting. If a star is orbiting an invisible object that is revealed to have more than ten times the mass of the Sun, then the object may be a black hole. Many such examples have been discovered. These strange pairs probably evolved when two stars formed together—one of them relatively "normal" and the other a huge body with up to perhaps fifty times the mass of the Sun. The latter exploded as a supernova, and the resulting neutron star collapsed into a black hole.

The second way to detect a black hole is to detect radiation from the gas that is falling into it. As infalling gas gets close to the black hole and its tremendous gravitational field, it is accelerated to speeds approaching that of light itself. The speeding atoms of gas collide violently with one another, creating heat. This reaches extremely high temperatures, so high that much of the radiation emitted is in the form of ultraviolet light, or even gamma rays and X-rays. When astronomers discover an unusually powerful source of gamma rays or X-rays, they suspect the presence of a black hole. If both clues are there—orbital motion of a star around an invisible, extremely massive body that is also a powerful source of X-rays—the chances that a black hole is present is very strong.

Even if we were to travel to the vicinity of a black hole, we would not be able to see it directly, since no light can escape from its surface. We might see, however, a glowing disk of gas and dust spiraling into it, glowing brighter and brighter the closer it comes to the black hole. Just before the material disappears forever, the blaze becomes intolerably intense as the radiation slips from visible light into the ultraviolet spectrum and then into the invisible spectrum of gamma rays and X-rays that lies beyond human vision.

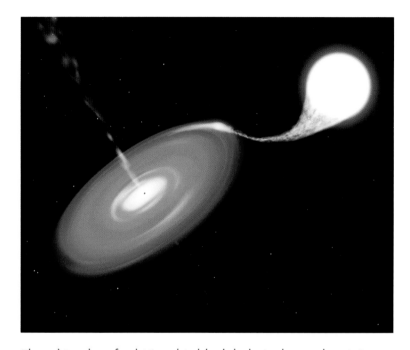

The white dwarf orbiting this black hole is doomed as it is being slowly drained into the black hole's bottomless gravity well. As matter swirls toward the center of the hole, its speed increases and it radiates more and more energy.

CHAPTER FOUR

AN INFINITE VARIETY

Stars come in an almost infinite variety, some of them so strange that at first glance you might not recognize them as stars at all. Stars certainly come in a wide range of sizes. There is a limit to just how small a star can be and still be a star. (We are not considering things like tiny white dwarfs or neutron stars here, which are merely the end products of a normal star's life.) A body with less than 8 percent of the mass of the Sun is simply too small for its gravity to generate enough heat at its core to trigger a nuclear reaction. On the other hand, an object with only 8 percent of the Sun's mass is still eighty times larger than the planet Jupiter. This is certainly big enough for a lot of heat to be generated in its core, even if it is not enough to start fusion. The surface temperature of an object like this may range from 1340°F to 3140°F (727°C to 1727°C). This means the object would glow with a dull red heat, like a hot coal.

A body such as this is called a **substellar object**, which means that it is not quite large enough to be a real star. Because it would glow only dully, it is also known as a **brown dwarf**. Until recently, the actual existence of brown dwarfs has been hypothetical. They would be much too small and dim to be seen through even a powerful telescope. However, many of the recent discoveries of extrasolar planets may have revealed the existence of brown dwarfs. The "planet" found orbiting the star Gliese 623 may in reality be a brown dwarf. Another brown dwarf may be orbiting VB8, a tiny, dim red star 21 light-years from the Sun. Only a few times larger than Jupiter, it has a surface temperature estimated to be about 2061°F (1127°C), so that it would glow with a dim red light.

Not all stars are spheres like our Sun. Altair, for instance, a bright, blue-white star, rotates once every six and a half hours.

This is a view from a planet orbiting a typical brown dwarf. The dully glowing object in the sky is a substellar object, too small to be a star, too large to be a true planet. Even though it is red hot, its source of heat is not the nuclear reactions that power normal stars. Instead, the heat is generated by its own gravitational contraction.

Altair, a star about 16 light-years from Earth, is remarkable for its high rate of rotation. Unlike the Sun, which rotates in 25 days, Altair rotates once every six and a half hours. As a result, the blue-white star is extremely flattened.

Rigel is an extremely bright, blue-white super giant. Its surface brightness is so great that it would be impossible even to glimpse with the naked eye. Here it is safely eclipsed by one of the moons of an imaginary planet, and Rigel's corona of hot gases is revealed. Wisps of red-glowing hydrogen gas have been blasted from the violent surface of the star.

Delta Cephei is a star that periodically changes its size. Every five days it increases in size by about 8 percent, doubling its brightness at the same time.

The Sun, by comparison, takes 25 days to make a rotation. The centrifugal forces created by Altair's extremely rapid rotation have caused the star to flatten out into a kind of lens shape. Pleione, one of the bright blue stars in the Pleiades cluster, rotates 100 times faster than the Sun, so that it is flattened nearly into a disk.

Neither are all stars as peaceful and as well-behaved as our Sun. Some stars vary greatly in brightness on a regular basis. Delta Cephei, a star about 1,000 light-years from the Sun, oscillates in size and brightness over a period of about five days. The increase in size is about 8 percent, and the increase in brightness is about 200 percent. These changes were first observed by the British astronomer John Goodricke in 1784. The star gave its name to all stars of this type, which are called **cepheid variables**. They are a quite important class of stars. Because the rate of pulsation is directly tied to the **absolute brightness** of the star—that is, the actual or intrinsic brightness—astronomers can observe the pulsation rate of any star of this type and use that to estimate its absolute brightness. Knowing that, they can then calculate the distance to the star. If a distant galaxy, for instance, contains cepheid variables, the distance of that galaxy can be determined very accurately.

Other stars vary in brightness due to enormous flares, or huge explosions, that erupt from their surfaces. Most **flare stars** are small, cool, red stars of low mass. Periodically, an outburst of hot gas will increase the brightness of the dim star. These flares may be similar to the flares we often observe erupting from the surface of our Sun.

The Cosmic Ballroom

Most stars come in pairs. In fact, of all the stars you can see in the sky, more than 55 percent have one or more companions. About 45 percent are double stars, 10 percent triple stars, and a handful consists of systems of four, five, six, or more members. At least one astronomer has suggested that the Sun itself might be part of a binary pair, with its partner being a small, dim red dwarf orbiting at a vast distance. Several astronomers have searched for the Sun's companion star, but to no avail.

In 1834, the German astronomer Friedrich Wilhelm Bessel noticed that the brightest star in the night sky, Sirius, behaved very oddly. Its motion through the sky seemed erratic. Instead of moving in a straight line, it wobbled ever so slightly. So slightly, in fact, that it took 50 years for each of the waves to complete. Bessel realized that by itself a star could not move in this way, but it would if it had an invisible companion. This companion would have to be dense enough for its gravitational pull to affect the course of the larger star. The orbit of the unseen companion star was calculated very exactly, but it stubbornly refused to be seen even through the most powerful telescope.

In 1862, American telescope-maker Alvan Clark tried out a new instrument by training it on Sirius, and discovered a tiny speck of light right beside the brilliant star. He realized that this was the long-sought companion. It was designated Sirius B. Because it must have about the same mass as the Sun but was so dim and hard to see, it was assumed that Sirius B was a cool, red star, and the whole matter was shelved as a mystery solved.

Most stars are members of binary teams, such as this pair of red giants.

Although we are used to thinking of stars being individuals because our own Sun appears to be a lone star, this is not usually the case. Most stars we see in the sky are parts of **multiple star** systems revolving around a common center of mass. (If there are just two stars in the system, it is called a **binary star** system.) To imagine what this means, picture a pair of bowling balls attached by a solid rod. If you set the pair spinning, they will spin around their common center of mass, the **barycenter**, which would be halfway between them. If the balls are mismatched however—for instance, if one was twice as massive as the other—the barycenter will move toward the heavier ball. If the larger ball is massive enough, the barycenter will fall somewhere

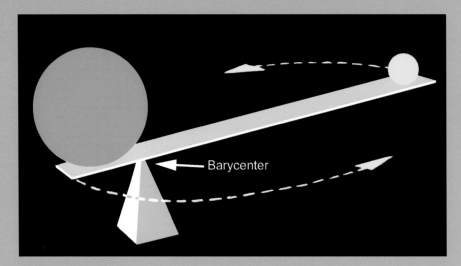

Barycenter

When two objects, such as a pair of stars, orbit each other, they circle a point between their centers of gravity called the barycenter. If the two stars are the same size, this point will be halfway between them. If they are of unequal size, the point will be closer to the large star.

(44)

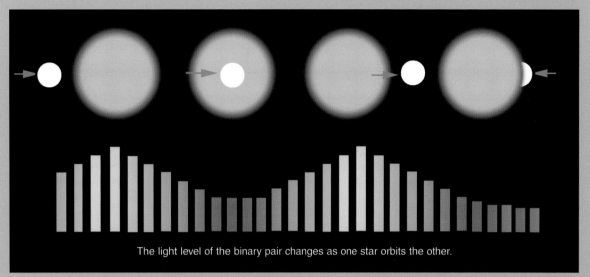

The light level of the binary pair changes as one star orbits the other.

As the smaller star orbits the larger one, it will sometimes pass in front of and sometimes behind the large star. This causes variations in the total amount of light emitted by the pair. This variation can be detected by astronomers, and it tells them that they have discovered a binary star system.

inside it. (This is the case with Earth and the Moon; their common center of mass lies beneath the surface of the Earth.)

Some multiple star systems can be discovered by direct observation. That is, the stars in the system can be seen in a telescope and their movements around one another measured. In most cases, however, where the companion star or stars are too dim to be seen, less direct methods must be used. One way is to look for unusual movement in a star. In the example of the mismatched bowling balls, if the smaller ball were invisible you would still be able to deduce its presence because of the wobbling motion the larger ball would have while the system was spinning. A wobbling motion like this in a star means that there is at least one companion.

Another way to locate multiple star systems is to look for regular variations in the level of light coming from the visible star. As the smaller star orbits the larger one, it will add its brightness to the total output when it is alongside the other star. But when it passes directly behind or in front of the larger star, the overall brightness will dim. By charting these regular variations, astronomers can determine not only the orbit of the invisible companion, but its size and spectral class as well.

(45)

Our eyes are shielded from the
brilliant light of Sirius by a
Saturn-like planet. This enables
us to see the dim companion star
in the distance at the upper right.

Mira Ceti, seen here from an imaginary planet, is a red giant about 400 times the size of the Sun. In the distance is Mira Ceti's bluish companion star.

In 1915, however, it was discovered that Sirius B was much stranger than anyone had previously thought. Instead of being a cool red body, it turned out that it was actually extremely hot—with a surface temperature of 44,540°F (24,732°C) as compared with the Sun's 10,832°F (6000°C)—and glowing a very bright white. The mystery was this: In order to appear as dim as it did yet have such a great gravitational influence on Sirius, Sirius B had to be very, very small and very, very massive. In fact, astronomers were astonished to discover that Sirius B was a tiny object about the size of Earth—into which was packed a mass equal to that of the Sun! This made Sirius B very dense, so dense that the amount it would take to fill a matchbox would weigh 50 tons. Sirius B was the first example of a white dwarf star discovered.

Since that discovery, it was found that white dwarfs are in fact rather common and that many stars have white dwarf companions. Procyon, for instance, is a yellowish star about twice the size of our Sun that is orbited by a white dwarf, and Omicron[2] Eridani is a binary system composed of a dim red star with a white dwarf companion.

There are many other possible combinations. Mira Ceti is a red giant star 400 times larger than our Sun and is orbited by a small, bluish companion. Antares is another red giant that is orbited by a tiny blue star, as is Betelgeuse. In the case of Betelgeuse, however, its companion may have such an elliptical orbit that the little star will actually pass through the giant star's thin atmosphere at its closest approach.

W Ursae Majoris is what is known as a **close binary**. These are stars that orbit so near each other that they are literally touch-

W Ursae Majoris is a close binary, where two white stars—each slightly larger and more massive than the Sun—orbit each other so closely that their atmospheres touch. Their eight-hour spin has flattened the stars into egg shapes.

Planets orbiting multiple star systems would present many unusual sights. This view is from a world orbiting a red star and a blue one. The starlight creates multicolored shadows from the rocks, red on one side and blue on the other.

ing. In the case of W Ursae Majoris, two hot white stars, each slightly more massive and larger than the Sun, orbit so closely that they share a common atmosphere. They whirl around their common center in a dizzying eight hours. The gravity of each star has warped the other into a kind of egg shape. Close binaries may form when a single star splits into two lobes during the very early days of its formation.

Castor, the second-brightest light in the constellation Gemini, is actually a system of six stars: three sets of double stars all orbiting around each other. Each pair of stars orbits one another so closely that they nearly touch. One pair, Castor A, the brightest stars in the system, are two bright, blue-white stars. Orbiting these are two smaller, reddish stars called Castor B. It takes the Castor B system 400 years to orbit Castor A. About 1,000 **astronomical units**

This view is from an imaginary planet orbiting near the faintest and most outlying of Castor's three binaries. This pair of low-mass red dwarf stars, Castor C, is 1,000 AU from the other four stars. They are flare stars, which periodically erupt with brilliant outbursts of energy. In the distance at the upper right are the other two pairs, Castor A and Castor B.

Most of the whitish light that we see from the Capella system comes from a close pair of stars. A second pair of faint, red stars orbits the first pair. The view shown here is from a planet that is orbiting the binary red stars. The second red star is above the near one. Just above the nearest star are the two hot, white stars, which orbit too close together to be distinguished from each other at this distance.

(AU) away from Castor A and B is the Castor C pair: two dim red dwarf stars that take 10,000 years to orbit the main system.

Capella is a system of four stars in the northern constellation of Auriga. The main pair is two large stars about three times as massive as the Sun. They are orbited by a pair of small, faint red stars that have only a few tenths the mass and radius of the Sun.

Stranger Pairs

In some binary systems, the stars do more than just orbit one another. They orbit so closely that they interact. We already saw an example of this in W Ursae Majoris, where two stars share a com-

mon atmosphere. In the binary system of Zeta Piscium, a hot, white star orbits a larger red star. Gas expelled from the larger star flows into a ring around the smaller one.

U Geminorum is a close binary pair consisting of a large, relatively cool red star and a smaller, hot blue one. The small star is so close to the large one that it orbits it in just four and a half hours. As gas is drawn from the red star, it falls into a glowing ring around the blue star. Enormous eruptions occur as gas from the ring is drawn onto the surface of the hotter, blue star. When these happen, the star increases its brightness by nearly 100 times. The process is similar to how novas are thought to occur, though

Zeta Piscium is one of many examples of mismatched binaries. In this case, one of the stars is feeding off the other. As mass flows from one star, it forms a ring around the other.

U Geminorum is a binary pair of very closely orbiting stars. Mass drawn from the large red star has formed a ring around its bluish companion.

SS 433 is one of the strangest star systems known. Material from the massive, hot star in the foreground is flowing toward an ultra-dense object—which may be a black hole or neutron star—where it forms a rapidly rotating disk. As the material falls into the object, two jets of ionized gas are blasted in opposite directions at a quarter of the speed of light.

the eruptions in the U Geminorum system occur on a more or less regular basis, about 100 days apart.

In the SS 433 system, gas from a red giant star flows into a disk circling the black hole that the star is orbiting. As the gas falls into the black hole at nearly the speed of light, it generates two beams of intense energy that jet at one quarter of the speed of light from opposite poles of the black hole. No other star is known to behave like this.

CHAPTER FIVE

BETWEEN THE STARS

The great spaces that lie between the stars are not empty. They are filled with dust and gas—mostly hydrogen. It is suspected by many astronomers that most of the normal matter in the universe takes the form of dark, invisible dust and gas. Because it is dark and thinly scattered, this matter is invisible to observers on Earth. There are places, however, where this dust and gas accumulate in great clouds, called nebulae. Many of these clouds glow in beautiful colors. Some clouds may be illuminated by the light of nearby stars in much the same way that clouds at sunset on Earth are illuminated by the Sun. Other clouds glow because the atoms that make them up are excited by the radiation from a nearby star. The atoms give off light just as do the atoms of gas in a neon tube when they are excited by the electric current passing through them. Other clouds are visible only as dark silhouettes against the stars and glowing nebulae in the background.

The beautiful Veil Nebula is a remnant of an ancient supernova. (NOAO/ AURA/NSF)

The Ghosts of Dead Stars

Where do the nebulae come from? Some are the remnants of supernovas—stars that have blasted their atmospheres into the universe in titanic explosions. When this occurs, the gas is expelled in a kind of vast bubble, expanding farther and farther from the doomed star. From Earth, this bubble often looks like a ring surrounding the star. Light and radiation from the star will cause the gas to glow in beautiful, delicate colors, and the nebula

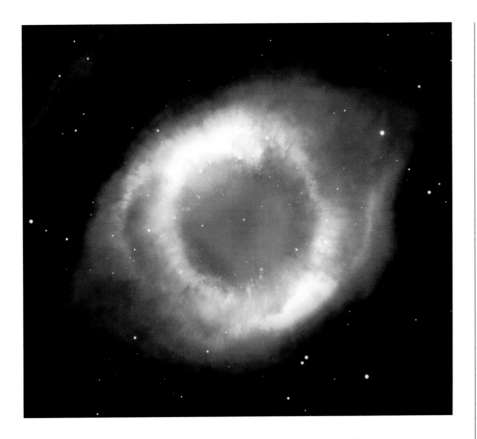

The beautiful Helix Nebula is the remnant of an exploding star. All that remains of the original star is the white dwarf that sits in the center of the vast bubble of gas it blew off in a titanic explosion some 10,000 years ago. The colors are created by radiation from the central star causing the gases in the nebula to glow.

can often take on fantastic shapes, but they are—at least on a galactic timetable—short-lived. The shell will continue to expand and grow thinner until it finally dissipates entirely and vanishes.

Most of the nebulae astronomers have observed are only a few tens of thousands of years old—and may last only another few tens of thousands of years. Not all such nebulae are so ancient, of course, since supernovas are always occurring.

The Crab Nebula was created less than 500 years ago, when a star detonated in a supernova. This was the "guest star" witnessed by Tycho Brahe, Chinese astronomers, and American Indian observers. (Jay Gallagher/WIYN/ NOAO/NSF)

The supernova that created the Crab Nebula, for instance, was observed in the year 1054 by Chinese astronomers and possibly even Native Americans. Expanding at the rate of 600 miles per second (966 km/sec), it has been growing larger every year since. At the center of the nebula is a pulsar, about 6 miles (10 km) in diameter, rotating thirty times a second. This is all that is left of the original star.

The material that the supernova has thrown into space will reenter the mixing bowl of gas and dust that will, eventually, contribute to the making of new stars. The thousands of supernova remnants in our galaxy contribute enough material every year to create five new stars.

A close-up of gas and dust clouds in the Omega Nebula shows small, dark, tight knots that may eventually become stars.

Stellar Nurseries

The nebulae left behind by exploding stars are only a tiny part of the vast quantities of gas and dust that swirl among the stars in our galaxy. This dust and gas is thin—thinner than a laboratory vacuum—but there is so much of it throughout the galaxy that there is enough to form billions of stars.

In many places throughout the Milky Way, this dust and gas has accumulated into huge, dark clouds. We can see these clouds

Stellar nurseries in the Large Magellanic Cloud: These masses of dust and gas are the raw material of stars. As gravity draws the dust and gas into clumps and knots, some may become dense enough for nuclear reactions to be triggered in their cores. When this happens, a star will be born.

(57)

only when they are illuminated by nearby stars or silhouetted against a background of bright stars. These vast masses of material are the nurseries where stars are born. One of the best-known of these is the beautiful Orion Nebula. Instead of being a dark, nearly invisible cloud of dust and gas, it is brightly lit by the young stars to which it is giving birth. It is a virtual star factory, filled with stars in every stage of evolution, from tiny, dark knots resembling springtime buds on a tree, to infant stars whose atomic furnaces were ignited only a few thousand years ago. Many of these young stars are surrounded by disks of dark material, making them look something like Frisbees. These may be **proto-planetary disks**—disks of dust and gas that may someday form a system of planets around these stars. Even though not all of these disks may evolve into solar systems—many will dissipate or be absorbed into their central stars—there are so many that astronomers believe that stars with planetary systems may be more common throughout the galaxy than anyone had originally thought.

Facing Page: The central part of the Orion Nebula contains one of the most active "stellar nurseries" known. (Bill Schoening/ NOAO/AURA/NSF)

CHAPTER SIX
THE MILKY WAY

All of the stars we can see in the sky are part of the Milky Way galaxy, a vast collection of 200 to 400 billion stars, swirling together like cream stirred into a cup of hot coffee. If we were able to see all of the Milky Way at once from some vast distance beyond it, it would resemble a fried egg—a bulbous center surrounded by a thick, flat disk. The disk, we would see, is composed of graceful, ghostly arms that spiral out from the central bulge like a pinwheel.

Buried deep within one of those spiral arms, about two thirds of the way from the central bulge, is the Sun and its solar system. Like every other star in the Milky Way, it orbits around the center of the galaxy, taking about 250 million years to make a single trip. In galactic years, then, Earth is only about sixteen years old.

A typical spiral galaxy, seen from a planet in one of the globular clusters that swarm around the galaxy. The concentration of older stars in the center of the galaxy gives the hub a reddish tint.

Needed: A large bowl, water, food coloring, a large spoon

The Milky Way is a spiral galaxy. The spiral arms are the result of nebulae and star clusters that are being dispersed as they move in their orbits around the hub of the galaxy. You can make a model of the galaxy that shows how the spiral arms form.

Fill the bowl with water, then stir it gently in just one direction with the spoon, so that the water is spinning in the bowl. (Another way to get the water to spin evenly is to place the bowl on a lazy Susan. Rotate the lazy Susan several times and then stop it. The water will continue to rotate.) Place a single drop of food coloring in the center of the rotating water. The central region of the colored water will be rotating rapidly while more slowly moving spiral arms will uncoil around it. This resembles our galaxy, but only if all of the stars in it had formed at the same time, just as your model galaxy formed all at once when you dropped the food coloring into the water. But the stars in the Milky Way did not form all at the same time.

Empty the bowl and fill it with clean water again. Stir it so that it starts spinning. This time, dribble a few tiny drops of food coloring at a time into the water, at different distances from the center. Each drop represents a different instance of star formation. Each drop will form its own spiral arm, the length and speed of its rotation depending on its distance from the center.

This shows why our galaxy has been able to keep its spiral form. If all of its stars had formed at one time, the galaxy's rotation would have "wound up" the arms like string on a spool. But with new nebulae and star-forming regions constantly appearing, the galaxy has been able to remain a spiral for billions of years.

You can see our galaxy if you make a trip out into the country on a dark night. Since we are within it, we see it edge-on, so it appears to be a broad band stretching from one side of the horizon to the other. This resemblance to a pale, ghostly stream in the sky earned it the name Milky Way (in fact, the word galaxy comes from a Greek word meaning "milk"). To the ancient Chinese, it looked like a river.

The Milky Way is a beautiful river of stars when seen in the dark, clear sky of the open country. The dark rifts in the Milky Way are caused by clouds of dark dust and gas obscuring our view of the stars behind them.

Looking toward the constellation Sagittarius, you are looking at the central bulge of the Milky Way. This would no doubt be a spectacular sight but for the fact that clouds of dark dust and gas obscure the view. The particular arm of the galaxy in which our Sun lies is called the Orion Arm. If you look in the direction of the constellation Orion, you will notice that the Milky Way seems a little brighter there. That is because you are looking right down the length of the spiral arm.

The Milky Way is huge. It spans 100,000 light-years from edge to edge. This means that even if you could travel at the incredible

The thick lanes of dark dust that lie in the plane of a typical spiral galaxy are clearly visible in this edge-on view of the galaxy known only as NGC 4013. Similar dark lanes of dust in our own galaxy are visible to the naked eye in the form of starless rifts.

speed of light—186,000 miles per second (300,000 km/sec)—it would still take 100,000 years to make the trip from one side of the galaxy to the other. The total mass of the galaxy is a trillion times the mass of the Sun. The central bulge—which is shaped like a slightly flattened sphere—appears distinctly pinkish-yellow because it is composed mostly of billions of old stars. The disk surrounding it is made of even more billions of stars, as well as dust and gas—mostly hydrogen and helium. Swirling around the entire galaxy, like a swarm of bees, is a roughly spherical collection of small clusters of 10,000 to a million stars, called **globular clusters**.

Our galaxy has at least four main arms. Each arm is composed of many individual star clouds and "mini-arms," such as the Orion Arm, in which the Sun lies. The Orion Arm is actually just a connection between a large inner arm—the Sagittarius Arm—and the next large outer arm—the Perseus Arm. The Orion Arm is about 28,000 light-years from the center of the galaxy.

The arms of the galaxy are composed of young stars, diffuse nebulae, and masses of **dark matter**—cold hydrogen gas laced with dust. You can see some of this material in the form of dark holes and rifts when you look at the Milky Way in a dark night sky. Most of the dust, however, lies in a thick, broad ring that surrounds the central bulge from 10,000 to 16,000 light-years from the center of the galaxy. This ring contains an amount of gas and dust equal to more than a billion Suns. It is called the **molecular ring**, because most of the material of which it is composed is in the form of individual molecules. This vast repository of raw materials is a stellar nursery, regularly giving birth to millions of brand-new stars.

As the young universe evolved, shortly after the Big Bang, it was filled with undifferentiated matter—that is, matter that had not yet formed into objects such as stars and galaxies. This matter first took the form of large clouds of gas, which eventually collected into dense clumps under the force of their own gravity. These clumps became nurseries for star formation. Since the stars in these clumps of gas were forming near one another, they evolved into clusters much like the globular clusters we see orbiting the Milky Way today. These small clusters eventually merged into larger ones. After enough time, these small galaxies collided with one another, merging into the large, mature galaxies of the present day, such as the Milky Way.

Collisions and mergers that took place early in the evolution of the universe were much more common then simply because the universe was more densely packed with material. As clusters merged to form small galaxies, and small galaxies merged to form large ones, there were fewer and fewer objects left, so that today a collision between galaxies is a relatively rare event.

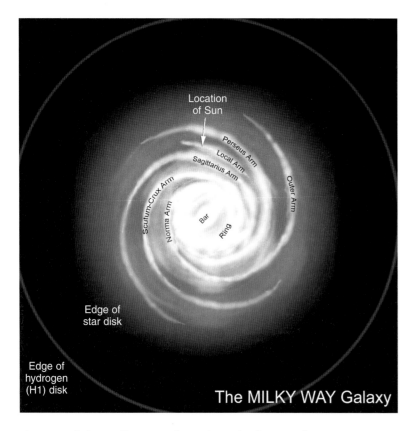

Location
of Sun

Perseus Arm

Local Arm

Sagittarius Arm

Outer Arm

Scutum-Crux Arm

Norma Arm

Bar

Ring

Edge of
star disk

Edge of
hydrogen
(H1) disk

The MILKY WAY Galaxy

A map of the Milky Way based on the latest information
gathered by optical and radio astronomers.

Journey to the Center of the Galaxy

The spiral arms curl out from the huge central bulge at the middle of the galaxy. Seen from above, the central bulge is flanked by a pair of broad extensions that form a bar 15,000 light-years long and 5,000 light-years wide. The bar—a feature the Milky Way shares with many other galaxies—may have been caused by a close approach of the Large Magellanic Cloud, one of two small satellite galaxies that orbit the Milky Way. Repeated close encounters with the Large Magellanic Cloud have stirred up the stars in the central bulge, causing them to take the form of a bar. If the Milky Way is indeed a barred galaxy, then its spiral arms would begin from the ends of the bars, like water spraying from the ends of a spinning lawn sprinkler.

An area around the center, about 1,000 light-years wide, contains vast quantities of dust and gas as well as huge numbers of red giant stars. Within 100 light-years of the core are crowded 60 million stars, along with dust and hydrogen gas. Some of this gas forms 100 light-year-long streamers a few light-years wide that stretch in huge, curved arcs above and below the plane of the galaxy. These are probably caused by intense magnetic fields at the core of the galaxy, in much the same way that iron filings will outline the field lines of a magnet.

Within ten light-years of the center is a crude, three-armed spiral shape, which is probably material flowing into the core. Within just a few light-years of the center, a few million stars swarm like bees in a hive. These stars—which are mostly red giants—are crammed as closely as people in a crowded elevator.

Most of the matter in the universe is dark matter—matter that does not emit light as stars do. Since it cannot be seen, dark matter is detected by the effect it has on the matter that we can see. For instance, it affects the motions of stars and galaxies. Imagine a magnet hidden under a sheet of cardboard. If you roll a steel ball across the cardboard, the magnet will cause the path of the ball to swerve from a straight line. Although you cannot see the magnet, you can deduce its presence from the action of the rolling ball. In the same way, astronomers can deduce the presence of dark matter by observing the action of stars and galaxies that cannot be explained any other way.

Even if there were not direct evidence for the existence of dark matter, astronomers would have to assume its presence to account for the formation of such large-scale structures as galaxies and clusters of galaxies. Astronomers have discovered that the amount of mass required to explain the existence and movements of these objects is much more than can be explained by the luminous matter that can be seen. They therefore infer the existence of dark matter in the universe.

There is a lot of dark matter in the universe. Although astronomers disagree on the exact amount, as much as 88 percent of the universe around us is made of this invisible matter. What is this dark matter, exactly? It can be any matter that does not emit light, such as planets like Earth and Jupiter. But astronomers believe most of it is probably subatomic particles. Whatever dark matter turns out to be, it is the dominant source of gravitational forces in the universe, so it is largely responsible for the structure of the universe we see around us today.

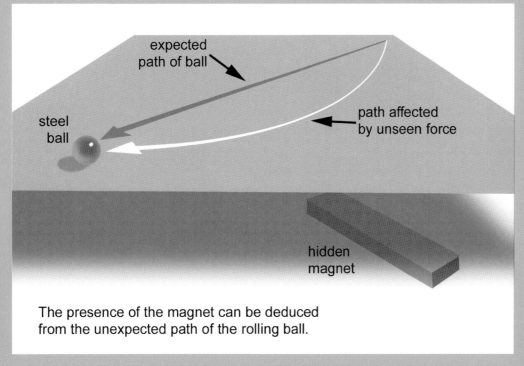

expected
path of ball

steel
ball

path affected
by unseen force

hidden
magnet

The presence of the magnet can be deduced
from the unexpected path of the rolling ball.

A planet orbiting a star near the center
of the Milky Way would have a sky
filled with suns. There would be no such
thing as night on this world, for as one
sun sets, another would be rising.

Whereas the nearest star to the Sun is 4.3 light-years away, these stars are separated by only 2 percent of a light-year—a distance only thirty times that of Pluto from the Sun. The sky here is filled with thousands of huge red stars, each as bright as a full moon.

Plunging even farther into the center of the galaxy, we find an object that may be only the size of Jupiter's orbit. No one knows for sure just what this object is or what lies at the very center of the galaxy. Astronomers are prevented from seeing the center by the masses of dark dust and gas that lie between the Sun and the center. They must depend on observations by radio telescopes and infrared astronomy to tell us what we know about the core of the galaxy. These observations have suggested that an enormous black hole may sit in the center of the Milky Way. The extremely high velocities of stars and gas orbiting the center hint at the presence of a massive gravitational source there, a source so massive that it could only be a black hole. Astronomers have calculated that this black hole—named Sagittarius A*—is probably 2 to 3 million times as massive as the Sun. Feeding on gas spiraling in from the molecular ring and the occasional unlucky star, the energy that the black hole would release would easily account for the vast outpouring of energy from the center of the galaxy.

Around the Milky Way

The Milky Way galaxy is surrounded by a spherical halo consisting of individual stars and about 150 globular clusters. These clusters are thought to have been formed during the early formation of the galaxy and contain some of the very oldest stars

This is a globular cluster seen from an icy planet circling one of its outermost stars. The stars appear orange-yellow because most of them are very old.

known. The halo is also filled with a very diffuse, hot, highly ionized gas.

While the stars in the galactic disk are in orbit around the hub, the stars and globular clusters of the halo are in randomly oriented elliptical orbits. This means that these stars and clusters will periodically dive through the disk and nucleus. A typical globular cluster may take as long as 200 million years to circle the galaxy once.

In addition to the halo, the Milky Way is also orbited by at least fourteen small satellite galaxies—so-called **dwarf galaxies**, because of their small size. The two largest of these, the Magellanic Clouds, are relatively small, ragged objects only a fraction the size of the Milky Way. Compared to the hundreds of billions of stars in our galaxy, the Large Magellanic Cloud—which is about 150,000 light-years from the Sun—contains only about 15 billion stars, while the Small Magellanic Cloud—about 200,000 light-years away—contains just 5 billion. They are named after the Portuguese navigator Ferdinand Magellan, who first observed them during his around-the-world voyage in 1521.

The Magellanic Clouds reside within an enormous river of hydrogen gas, called the Magellanic Stream, that loops around our galaxy. Several other tiny satellite galaxies also have orbits that lie within the stream. The Magellanic Stream is made up of several clouds connected by tendrils of thinner gas.

Some of the nearer dwarf galaxies are being disrupted by the powerful gravitational field of the Milky Way. The nearest of these, the Canis Major Dwarf Galaxy, is only about 45,000 light-years from the center of the galaxy (and about 25,000 light-years from

Although Andromeda was known to astronomers as long ago as the tenth century, no one suspected its true nature. The Persian astronomer Abd-al-Rahman Al-Sufi called it the "Little Cloud," in the *Book of Fixed Stars*, which he wrote in 964. The first telescopic description of it was made by German astronomer Simon Marius in 1612, and in 1764 French astronomer Charles Messier added it to his great catalog, from which it got its official designation of M31. It was assumed to be merely one more of the many nebulae that astronomers had discovered, all of which are nearby features of our own galaxy.

British astronomer William Herschel, who had developed one of the first theories about the true nature of the Milky Way galaxy, suggested that Andromeda might, like the Milky Way, be an independent island universe. He estimated its distance to be "2,000 times the distance of Sirius," or 17,200 light-years. He guessed its diameter at 850 times the distance of Sirius and its thickness at 155 times—7,310 and 1,333 light-years respectively. In reality, the distance to Andromeda is 2,300,000 light-years, and its diameter is about 200,000 light-years.

In 1864, William Huggins compared the spectra of gaseous nebulae with that of Andromeda and found that Andromeda's spectrum was much more like that of a star than of a gaseous object. The spiral nature of Andromeda was first revealed in the photographs taken in 1887 by British astronomer Isaac Roberts.

American astronomer Edwin Hubble (1889–1953) found the first Cepheid variable in Andromeda in 1923. For the first time not only was the distance to Andromeda known accurately, but so was its true nature as an independent galaxy similar to our own Milky Way.

The giant Andromeda galaxy appears in this image created by NASA's Galaxy Evolution Explorer satellite. Andromeda is the most massive member of the local group of galaxies that includes the Milky Way and is the nearest large galaxy to our own.

the Sun). This small galaxy was not discovered until 2003. Most of the matter of which it was composed is being scattered along its orbit as the Milky Way tears it apart.

The Local Group

The Milky Way galaxy and its satellites are members of a much larger neighborhood of galaxies known as the **Local Group**. It has more than thirty members, including the Milky Way. In addition to our galaxy, the other major member is the Andromeda galaxy (M31), with third place being taken by the Triangulum galaxy (M33). All three are giant spiral galaxies, of which the Milky Way is by far the most massive. Almost all of the rest are small satellite galaxies of either the Milky Way or Andromeda. The small remainder float freely in the Local Group.

The galaxies that form the Local Group are not isolated, but locked together by their mutual gravitation. The Andromeda galaxy is so large and nearby that it can be seen with the naked eye. It has been known to astronomers for more than a thousand years, though it was not until the twentieth century that its true nature was known. It is near—"only" 2.4 to 2.9 million light-years away—and it lies so open to view that Andromeda has been closely studied as a slightly larger, less massive model of our own galaxy. Because the Milky Way and Andromeda are approaching each other at about 62 miles per second (100 km/sec), some astronomers have speculated that the two galaxies may collide and merge in some distant future to form a single giant elliptical galaxy.

M 110 and M 32 are small, elliptical satellite galaxies of Andromeda

The Andromeda galaxy is about 2.9 million light-years from the Sun.

M31 Andromeda

M 110

M 32

NGC 147
NGC 185

Globular clusters

NGC 278

NGC 147 and NGC 185 are a pair of dwarf elliptical companion galaxies to the Andromeda galaxy. Perspective makes them appear close to our galaxy. NGC 278 is a much more distant elliptical galaxy.

The Sun

Milky Way